THE GREAT PHILOSOPHERS

Consulting Editors
Ray Monk and Frederic Raphael

BERKELEY

David Berman

Published in 1999 by
Routledge
29 West 35th Street
New York, NY 10001

First published in 1997 by
Phoenix
A Division of the Orion Publishing Group Ltd.
Orion House
5 Upper Saint Martin's Lane
London WC2H 9EA

10 9 8 7 6 5 4 3 2 1

Library of Congress Cataloging-in-Publication Data

Berman, David, 1942–
        Berkeley / David Berman.
          p. cm.—(The great philosophers : 12)
        Includes bibliographical references.
        ISBN 0-415-92387-5 (pbk.)
        1. Berkeley, George, 1685–1753. I. Title. II. Series:
        Great Philosophers (Routledge (Firm)) : 12.
B1348.B457 1999
192—dc21   99-21673
                                                             CIP

CONTENTS

To Patricia and Hannah Bella

BERKELEY

Experimental Philosophy

BERKELEY: EXPERIMENTAL PHILOSOPHY

George Berkeley, it is generally agreed, was an empiricist philosopher; that is, he regarded experience as forming the basis of all human knowledge. As he classically put it in his *Principles of Human Knowledge* (1710) § 3: *'esse* is *percipi'*, to be is to be perceived. My aim in this volume is to examine Berkeley's empiricism by looking closely at the specific experiences and experiments he used to understand the world and everything in it. Seeing Berkeley's work in this way has, I shall try to show, two advantages: it gives us an overview of his writings and philosophy; it also shows one way in which his philosophy may be relevant today.

Berkeley's birth (1685) and education (BA 1704) coincided with one of the radiant periods in modern experimental science, two of whose jewels were Newton's *Principia Mathematica* (1687) and *Opticks* (1704). Like many philosophers of the time, Berkeley himself was actively engaged in the new scientific developments. He was a precocious and accomplished mathematician, as can be seen from his two earliest publications, *Arithmetica* and *Miscellanea Mathematica* (1707). On the whole, however, he was critical of mathematics, which he regarded as a science of empty abstractions. And it was in his later tract, *The Analyst* (1734), that he gave eloquent expression to his criticism by pointing out a serious flaw in Newton's theory of fluxions as well as drawing theological consequences from it.

The key science for Berkeley was not mathematics – as it was for Descartes and Leibniz – but psychology, the science of experience. Indeed, Berkeley's first major work, an *Essay Towards a New Theory of Vision* (1709), is regarded as a landmark not only in philosophy but also in psychology – as 'psychology's first monograph', according to some historians.[1] However, to say that Berkeley was a pioneer psychologist is not to imply that he was the first great philosopher either to contribute to psychology or to use it for philosophical ends. Where Berkeley was exceptional was in showing how the two disciplines could be successfully brought together. It was his fruitful union of philosophy and psychology that exerted a considerable impact on nineteenth-century British philosophy, and particularly on J. S. Mill, the leading figure of the period, who regarded Berkeley as 'the one of greatest philosophical genius'.[2]

And yet this view of Berkeley as the psychological philosopher *par excellence* can be easily lost sight of, because Berkeley has also been a revered figure of the so-called revolution in twentieth-century philosophy that displaced Mill's psychological vision of philosophy, or mental science, as it was often called. This revolutionary movement went through a number of phases, including logical atomism, logical positivism and linguistic philosophy, until it finally settled into what is now called analytic philosophy, which, in common with its antecedents, is centrally concerned with language and logic, conceptual analysis and argument, and also with the negative recognition that philosophy is not mental science.[3]

Berkeley, the mental scientist, did not fit into this non-psychological, analytic picture of philosophy. Yet, fortunately for his reputation, there was that other side of his work where he shows himself to be a master of conceptual analysis and argument, as well as being sensitive to the complexity and pathology of philosophical language. The two sides of Berkeley's work can be seen in his general Introduction to the *Principles of Human Knowledge*, his *magnum opus*. As John Locke's main work, the *Essay Concerning Human Understanding* (1690), begins with a critique of innatism, so Berkeley began his with what he considers to be even more fundamental, a critique of language, especially of abstract and general words. Berkeley's main target here is Locke, who, while believing that only particular things exist in the objective world, also held that we human beings are able to form abstract and general ideas, and that these are essential for reasoning and demonstration. Berkeley quotes Locke in §12 of the Introduction to the *Principles*, but it is §13 where he offers his choicest quotation and conceptual criticism:

> To give the reader a yet clearer view of the nature of abstract ideas, and the uses they are thought necessary to, I shall add one more passage out of [Locke's] *Essay on Human Understanding*, which is as follows. '*Abstract Ideas* are not so obvious or easy to children or the yet unexercized mind as particular ones. If they seem so to grown men, it is only because by constant and familiar

5

use they are made so. For when we nicely reflect upon them, we shall find that general ideas are fictions and contrivances of the mind, that carry difficulty with them ... For example, does it not require some pains and skill to form the general idea of a triangle (which is yet none of the most abstract comprehensive and difficult) for it must be neither oblique nor rectangle, neither equilateral, equicrural, nor scalenon, but *all and none* of these at once. In effect, it is something imperfect that cannot exist, an idea wherein some parts of several different and *inconsistent* ideas are put together ...' B.4. C.7. §9. [Now, comments Berkeley,] If any man has the faculty of framing in his mind such an idea of a triangle as is here described, it is in vain to pretend to dispute him out of it, nor would I go about it. All I desire is, that the reader would fully and certainly inform himself whether he has such an idea or no. And this, methinks, can be no hard task for anyone to perform. What more easy than for anyone to look a little into his own thoughts, and there try whether he has, or can attain to have, an idea that shall correspond with the description that is here given of the general idea of a triangle, which is, *neither oblique, nor rectangle, equilateral, equicrural, nor scalenon, but all and none of these at once? (§13)*

Berkeley's confidence that no one will be able to discover such an idea has two sources: (1) experience and (2) its flawed linguistic or conceptual character. It is the second of these which comes to the fore in §13, where Berkeley reveals the weakness in Locke's position, a weakness that we can easily see – once a Berkeley, like Sherlock Holmes, has pointed it out. When Dr Watson expresses astonishment at Sherlock Holmes's perspicacity, Holmes is famous for saying, 'Elementary, my dear Watson.' And Berkeley says something similar (in a somewhat different context) when he spoke of 'the obvious tho' Amazing truth ... tis no Witchcraft to see.' (PC, no. 279). Berkeley calls our attention to the obvious flaw in Locke's description of abstract ideas by simply italicizing its key phrases, such as 'all and none' and 'inconsistent'. Earlier, in the *New Theory of Vision*, he had driven this conceptual point home less gently when he asserted that 'the above-mentioned idea of a triangle', as described by Locke, 'is made up of manifest, staring contradictions' (§125). Yet even here, Berkeley has not abandoned his psychological approach, since he says in §125 that he has made 'reiterated endeavours to apprehend the general idea'; and that the reader must 'look into his own thoughts' to see whether he can attain the idea described by Locke.

But there is a problem here: why should Berkeley repeatedly try to apprehend 'something' which he has shown to be self-contradictory? For surely that which is self-contradictory cannot exist. The answer, I think, is that Berkeley believes that language is so flawed that it cannot be relied upon, not even when it appears to be revealing a contradiction. What can be trusted is experience, whether inner or outer. So the only reliable test for determining whether an abstract idea of triangle, or any abstract idea, exists is to try to experience it by introspection.

7

That Berkeley's main argument against Locke is psycho-logical or empirical, rather than linguistic or conceptual, can also be seen in §10 of the Introduction, where he writes:

Whether others have this wonderful faculty of abstract-ing their ideas, they best can tell: for myself I find indeed I have a faculty of imagining, or representing to myself the ideas of those particular things I have perceived and of variously compounding and dividing them. I can imagine a man with two heads or the upper parts of a man joined to the body of a horse. I can consider the hand, the eye, the nose, each by itself abstracted or separated from the rest of the body. But then whatever hand or eye I imagine, it must have some particular shape and colour. Likewise the idea of man that I frame to myself, must be either of a white, or a black, or a tawny, straight, or crooked, a tall, or a low, or a middle-sized man. I cannot by any effort of thought conceive the abstract idea above described. And it is equally impossible for me to form the abstract idea of motion distinct from the body moving, and which is neither swift nor slow, curvilinear nor rectilinear; and the like may be said of all the other abstract general ideas whatsoever… And there are grounds to think most men will acknowledge themselves to be in my case. The generality of men which are simple and illiterate never pretend to abstract notions (§10)

Here we have Berkeley drawing mainly on his own experiences (or lack of them), but also on the (implicit) testimonies of most men. Further on, in §14, the empirical evidence Berkeley uses against the Lockean position is exclusively of the latter kind. Here his argument has two phases. In the first he draws attention to the fact that for most people talking is 'easy and familiar'. The second starts from the conscious awareness and memory of most adults and then moves to the observation of children:

> Much is ... said of the difficulty that abstract ideas carry with them, and the pains and skill requisite to the forming them. And it is on all hands agreed that there is need of great toil and labour of the mind, to emancipate our thoughts from particular objects, and raise them to those sublime speculations that are conversant about abstract ideas. From all which the natural consequence should seem to be, that so difficult a thing as the forming abstract ideas was not necessary for *communication* which is so easy and familiar to all sorts of men. But we are told, if they seem obvious and easy to grown men, *It is only because by constant and familiar use they are made so.* Now I would fain know at what time it is, men are employed in surmounting that difficulty, and furnishing themselves with necessary helps for discourse. It cannot be when they are grown up, for then it seems they are not conscious of any such pains-taking; it remains therefore to be the business of their childhood. And surely, the great and multiplied labour of framing abstract notions, will be found a hard task for that tender age. Is it not a hard thing to imagine that a couple of children cannot prate together, of their sugar plumbs

and rattles and the rest of their little trinkets, till they have first tacked together numberless inconsistencies, and so framed in their minds *abstract general ideas*, and annexed them to every common name they make use of? (§14)

However, the empirical data on which Berkeley mainly draws are his own subjective, first-person, introspective observations. As he bluntly puts it in a 1730 letter written in America: 'I cannot find I have any such [abstract] idea, and this is my reason against it.' (*Works* II, 293). For short, I call this Berkeley's subjective empiricism.

Subjective empiricism needs to be distinguished from objective empiricism, even though Berkeley makes abundant use of both in his work, and the difference for him is largely one of degree rather than kind. Thus for Berkeley, both what we perceive by our senses and what we perceive by looking inwards in our imagination and memory are all ideas; the former are simply more forceful, vivid, orderly and less subject to our wills, than the latter. Hence all experiences and experiments are essentially psychological: the former constitute the realm of objective empiricism, the latter that of subjective empiricism. However, objective empiricism does have another feature which is somewhat more problematic for Berkeley the idealist, but of which he nonetheless wishes to avail, namely, that it includes what other minds say they experience.

So while §10 is mainly in the realm of subjective empiricism, concerned with Berkeley's own introspective findings, §14 is almost exclusively objective, since it is based on the fact that most adults and children appear to use language in an easy way, and that adults do not report having gone through a painful period in their acquisition of abstract language and knowledge.

The empirical evidence that Berkeley assembles in §14 is not very specific. But this is not characteristic of his objective empiricism. Thus in *Alciphron, or the Minute Philosopher* (1732), his main defence of religion, Berkeley makes an appeal to experience that is both more specific and public. It is a counter-factual argument, aimed at defending the Mosaic or biblical chronology: that the world and human beings were created by God about 6,000 years ago. For, Berkeley argues, if people had been in the world for a significantly greater time – as some freethinkers claimed – then we should find durable objects, such as gems, utensils and medals, buried deep in the ground. But since no one, Berkeley maintains, has found such items, it follows that the world is most unlikely to be older than that calculated by Moses (Alc. VI. 23). Of course, Berkeley has been proved factually wrong, but not wrong in his empiricist methodology. He was in this instance – and this is not untypical – wrong for the right reasons, which may well be better than being right for the wrong reasons.

Berkeley's objective empiricism comes out in a more positive manner in the *Theory of Vision Vindicated* (1733), where he quotes from William Cheselden's 1728 account of a boy who was blind from infancy, but was enabled to see by the surgical removal of cataracts. Thus

Before I conclude, [Berkeley writes] it may not be amiss

to add the following extract from the *Philosophical Transactions* [no. 402, 1728], relating to a person blind from his infancy, and long after made to see: 'When he [the boy] first saw, he was so far from making any judgement about distances that he thought all objects whatever touched his eyes (as he expressed it) as what he felt did his skin ... He knew not the shape of any thing, nor any one thing from another, however different in shape or magnitude: but upon being told what things were, whose form he before knew from feeling, he would carefully observe that he might know them again: but having too many objects to learn at once, he forgot many of them: And (as he said) at first he learned to know, and again forgot, a thousand things in a day. Several weeks after he was couched, being deceived by pictures, he asked which was the lying sense, feeling or seeing? ... The room he was in, he said, he knew to be but part of the house, yet he could not conceive that the whole house could look bigger...' Thus [Berkeley concludes], by fact and experiment, those points of the theory which seem the most remote from common apprehension were not a little confirmed, many years after I had been led into the discovery of them by reasoning. (§71)

Berkeley takes this testimony as providing factual and experimental vindication of the main thesis of his *New Theory of Vision*, that what we see is entirely different from what we touch. So Berkeley is using publicly accessible material, the testimony of the boy as communicated by

Cheselden; although it is based on the experiences of the boy. Berkeley first mentioned Cheselden's corroboration in the second edition of *Alciphron*, where he noted that the 'paradoxes' of his *New Theory of Vision* were 'first received with great ridicule', but were 'surprisingly confirmed by a case of a person made to see who had been blind from his birth. See "Philos. Transact." number 402' (*Works* III, 161). On a small but significant point of accuracy, it will be noticed that Berkeley made one change from *Alciphron* to the *Theory of Vision Vindicated* in his description of the case, that is, he changed 'blind from his birth' to 'blind from his infancy'. Here he was bringing himself into line with Cheselden, although possibly weakening the force of his claim.

The objective empiricism shown in the quotation from Cheselden is not in any way unusual for Berkeley. For although he is best known for his theoretical reasoning and thought experiments, contained in his three famous philosophical works of 1709–13, his lesser-known works are pervaded by physical observations. Thus his first extant composition, the essay on the Cave of Dunmore (*Works* IV, 257–64) was a detailed description of a large cave in the vicinity of Kilkenny, where he attended school. Berkeley explored the cave about 1699 while a schoolboy, but he did not write up his account until 1706, when at university in Dublin – which suggests, given the essay's accurate detail, that he had a considerable capacity for vivid visual recollection, perhaps even for eidetic imagery and memory.

Berkeley's interest in external empirical observation is shown, too, in his first-hand observations and description

13

of an eruption of Mt Vesuvius, published in 1717 in the *Philosophical Transactions*, and his description of tarantulas in Italy, recorded in his 1717 travel notebooks. This aspect of Berkeley impressed some of his friends. Thus Thomas Blackwell, who knew Berkeley in Italy, wrote of him: 'He travelled through a great part of Sicily on foot, clambered over the mountains and crept into the caverns to investigate into its natural history, and discover the causes of its volcanoes; and I have known him sit for hours in forges and founderies to inspect their successive operations.'[4]

Berkeley's *Querist* (1735-7), his main work in economic theory, also contains considerable description of economic practices, particularly in Ireland. Yet here he goes further than natural history. In *Querist*, nos 46-7, he proposes the following thought experiment, with the aim of determining what basic economic forms of life will develop if sailors were marooned on an island:

> 46 Whether, in order to understand the true nature of wealth and commerce, it would not be right to consider a ship's crew cast upon a desert island, and by degrees forming themselves to business and civil life, while industry begot credit, and credit moved to industry?
> 47 Whether such men would not all set themselves to work? Whether they would not subsist by the mutual participation of each other's industry? Whether, when one man had in his way procured more than he could consume, he would not exchange his superfluities to supply his wants? Whether this must not produce credit? Whether, to facilitate these conveyances, to record, and

14

circulate this credit, they would not soon agree on certain tallies, tokens, tickets, or counters? (*Works* VI, 108–9)

But Berkeley's objective empiricism is most abundantly displayed in *Siris: A Chain of Philosophical Reflexions on Tar-Water* (1744), his last major work, written when he was Bishop of Cloyne in Ireland. Here, and in his subsequent writings on tar-water, he defends tar-water as a valuable, if not universal, medicine. To this end, he carefully describes tar in its various forms, the making of tar-water, his experiments with it and especially the physical effects that intensive drinking of tar-water had on himself, his family, neighbours, patients, and others who took tar-water at his recommendation.

In one of his later tar-water writings, the first *Letter to Thomas Prior on Tar-water* (1744), Berkeley also describes in some detail his empiricist methodology in his investigation of tar-water. In the beginning, he says, he started out with mere hearsay information about the medicinal value of tar (§14); from which he made some preliminary trials (§15), which, because they were successful, encouraged him to theorize about tar (§§15–17), which helped him to arrange more refined tests (§18). Now that he had a clear understanding of the medicine he believed was valuable, he 'tried many experiments' (§19), 'in many various and unlike cases' (§20). And it was on the basis of these experiments, rather than any theory, he says, that 'is founded my opinion of the salutary virtues of tar-water; which virtues are recommended from, and depend on, experiments and matters of fact, and neither stand nor fall with any theories or speculative principles whatsoever'. (§20)

Berkeley continued to be interested in the factual evidence for tar-water, as is shown in his last published essay, 'Farther Thoughts on Tar-water', which appeared in his *Miscellany* (1752), published a year before his death. Like his first extant essay of 1706, on the Dunmore cave, the 1752 essay is almost entirely given over to natural history description – in this case the successful cures brought about by tar-water. Berkeley also put forward here what may be one of the earliest proposals for a controlled medical experiment, to test tar-water's efficacy with smallpox:

> The experiment may be easily made if an equal number of poor patients in the small-pox were put into two hospitals at the same time of the year, and provided with the same necessaries of diet and lodging; and, for further care, let the one have a tub of tar-water and an old woman, the other hospital, what attendance and drugs you please. (*Works* V, 210)

The importance of physical experiment and observation is also evident in Berkeley's solution to the moon illusion in the *New Theory of Vision*. Why, in short, does the moon always appear larger on the horizon than it does in the meridian? Here we move away from natural science and back closer to philosophy. In this case, too, it is not a matter of many observations, but of seeing the significance of one familiar but crucial one. For while many notable thinkers, beginning with Ptolemy and including Descartes, Gassendi and Hobbes, had tried to solve the illusion, none of them before Berkeley had seemed to notice that the moon seen on the horizon was not merely enlarged, but that it varied considerably in size, sometimes appearing as enormous. This observation proved, according to Berkeley, that most of the earlier solutions could not be correct or entirely correct, since they supposed a constant, invariable cause, as in the case of Ptolemy's solution, more recently restated in 1688 by John Wallis, that it was the intervening land or sea mass on the horizon that made the moon look large and hence produced the illusion. But if Ptolemy and Wallis were right, then 'the moon appearing in the very same situation' (NTV, §77) should always be the same size – but it isn't.

Berkeley's own solution was, in the first instance, that it was the presence of more atmosphere or vapours on the surface of the earth that explains the illusion and its fluctuations. By diffusing the light coming from the moon, the atmosphere or vapours makes the moon appear fainter which, as a cue for size, makes the moon seem large to an observer. Since the presence of vapours is something that is intermittent and varies in intensity, it is able to explain the variation in the illusion (§68). However, in the final analysis, Berkeley thought it was a contextual or gestaltist matter, comparing it with the way the meaning of a word is often determined by its context:

> Now, it is known a word pronounced with certain circumstances, or in a certain context with other words, hath not always the same import and signification that it hath when pronounced in some other circumstances or

different context of words. [So] The very same visible appearance as to faintness and all other respects, if placed on high, shall not suggest the same magnitude that it would if it were seen at an equal distance on a level with the eye. (NTV, §73)

Berkeley also employs experiments to show that the previous solutions, such as those offered by Descartes and Ptolemy/Wallis, are incorrect. Thus if one blocks out surrounding objects, such as trees and chimneys (crucial in Descartes' solution), or the intervening land or sea mass (as in the Ptolemy/Wallis solution), by seeing the horizontal moon through a cylinder or over a wall, the illusion, Berkeley says, nonetheless persists. Hence these factors cannot be responsible for the illusion. But there is a problem with these blocking out experiments, namely that according to recent psychological findings, the illusion does *not* persist. Berkeley himself seems to have recognized this, although reluctantly, since he tends to qualify the experiments and his conclusions in subsequent editions of the *New Theory of Vision*; indeed, he entirely omits the cylinder experiment in later editions, although unlike his correction in the *Theory of Vision Vindicated* (see above), he never fully withdrew his initial (probably mistaken) claim – a claim to which he was probably led by William Moly-neux.[5]

Berkeley also uses some partly physical experiments in his *Principles* and *Three Dialogues between Hylas and Philo-nous* (1713) to support his idealism – that physical objects and their properties do not exist externally, but only in the

18

mind. Thus he notes that if one puts one hand in a hot and the other in a cold place, then plunges both in luke warm water, the water will feel cold to one hand, hot to the other, which seems show that the water in itself is neither hot nor cold (*Works* II, 178–9). Yet in *Principles*, §§14 and 15, where Berkeley first mentions these relativity experiments, he makes it entirely clear that 'this method of arguing', which was used by Locke and other advanced thinkers to prove the mind-dependence of secondary qualities, such as warmth and coldness, odours and tastes, 'doth not so much prove that there is no extension or colour in an outward object, as that we do not know by sense which is the true extension or colour of the object' (§15).

However, in the *Three Dialogues* Berkeley introduces an experiment that is neither sceptical nor relativistic and does show, according to him, that heat (and also cold, tastes and odours) is mind-dependent, and not in the outward object. When you feel something very hot, for example a fire, it feels painful; both the extreme heat and the pain 'are immediately perceived at the same time, and the fire affects you only with one simple, or uncompounded idea'. Therefore, since you cannot separate the pain from the extreme heat, the heat must exist – as the pain does – in the mind (*Works* II, 176). And this, Berkeley shows, can be applied equally to all degrees of heat – since a moderate warmth feels pleasurable, which is a subjective state – and also to cold and, *mutatis mutandis*, to tastes and odours.

The form of this experimental argument – that x (extreme heat) cannot be divided or subtracted from y (pain) – is also used even more generally by Berkeley in his more ambitious thought experiment in *Principles*, §10: '... I desire anyone to reflect and try, whether he can by any abstraction of thought, conceive the extension and motion of a body, without all other sensible qualities. For my own part, I see evidently that it is not in my power to frame an idea of a body extended and moved, but I must withal give it some colour or other sensible quality which is acknowledged to exist only in the mind.' Because one cannot perceive or conceive a body without some sensible or secondary quality, such as colour, that body must exist in the mind, along with the secondary quality.

In the *New Theory of Vision*, §43, Berkeley shows in detail how it is impossible to separate colour from an extended object. 'I appeal', he says,

> to any man's experience, whether the visible extension of any object doth not appear as near to him as the colour of that object; nay, whether they do not both seem to be in the very same place. Is not the extension we see coloured, and is it possible for us, so much as in thought, to separate and abstract colour from extension? Now, where the extension is there surely is the figure, and there the motion too.

Against Berkeley, it is sometimes asserted that sighted persons can perceive an extended yet non-coloured thing, such as glass; although it is not clear how they would know the glass was there. It has also been suggested by Jonathan Bennett that Berkeley and Hume were wrong, that a blind person can perceive or conceive an extended object without colour.[6] But this criticism overlooks Berkeley's phrase 'or other sensible quality' (PHK, §10), which, although he does not elucidate, almost certainly means sensible qualities such as smooth, rough, heat, cold, and feelings of pressure and resistance. The question will then be: can a blind person frame an idea of extended tangible body without one of these mind-dependent qualities?

Whereas the two previous experiments are about the impossibility of subtracting x from y, the following from *New Theory of Vision*, §131, is about the impossibility of adding x and y:

> ... it is, I think, an axiom universally received that quantities of the same kind may be added together and make one entire sum. Mathematicians add lines together: but they do not add a line to a solid, or conceive it as making one sum with a surface: these three kinds of quantity being thought incapable of any such mutual addition, and consequently of being compared together in the several ways of proportion, as by them esteemed intirely disparate and heterogeneous. Now let any one try in his thoughts to add a visible line or surface to a tangible line or surface, so as to conceive them making one continued sum or whole. He that can do this may think them homogeneous: but he that cannot, must by the foregoing axiom think them heterogeneous: A blue and a red line I can conceive added together into one sum and making one continued line: but to make in my thoughts one continued line of a visible and tangible line added together is, I find, a task far more difficult, and even insurmountable: and I

> leave it to the reflexion and experience of every particu-
> lar person to determine for himself.

Here and in the previous experiment we are moving further
from the objective to the subjective, that is, from physical
to thought experiments.

Probably Berkeley's most famous (and contentious)
thought experiment is summed up in the challenge: try to
think of an object existing unperceived. This is sometimes
called his master argument for his immaterialism, and is to
be found in the *Principles*, §22–3:

> ... It is but looking into your own thoughts, and so,
> trying whether you can conceive it possible for a sound,
> or figure, or motion, or colour, to exist without the mind
> or unperceived. This easy trial may make you see, that
> what you contend for is downright contradiction. Inso-
> much that I am content to put the whole upon this
> issue; if you can but conceive it possible for one
> extended moveable substance, or in general, for any one
> idea or anything like an idea, to exist otherwise than in a
> mind perceiving it, I shall readily give up the cause ... I
> shall grant you its existence, though you cannot either
> give me any reason why you believe it exists, or assign
> any use to it when it is supposed to exist ...
>
> 23   But say you, surely there is nothing easier than to
> imagine trees, for instance, in a park or books existing in
> a closet, and nobody by to perceive them. I answer, you
> may so, there is no difficulty in it: but what is all this, I
> beseech you, more than framing in your mind certain
> ideas which you call books and trees, and at the same

time omitting to frame the idea of anyone that may perceive them? But do not you yourself perceive or think of them all the while? This therefore is nothing to the purpose: it only shows you have the power of imagining or forming ideas in your mind; but it doth not shew that you can conceive it possible, the objects of your thought may exist without the mind: to make out this it is necessary that you conceive them existing unconceived or unthought of, which is a manifest repugnancy. When we do our utmost to conceive the existence of external bodies, we are all the while only contemplating our own ideas. But the mind taking no notice of itself, is deluded to think it can and doth conceive bodies existing unthought of or without the mind; though at the same time they are apprehended by or exist in itself.

This is Berkeley's more usual mode of experiment: division; try to divide your perception of a body (x) from that body itself (y). Berkeley sometimes states this as a conceptual point – a body unperceived or unthought of is contradictory – but more usually as an experimental one: *try* separating x and y. As he says in *Principles*, §6: 'To be convinced of which, the reader need only reflect and try to separate in his own thoughts the being of a sensible thing from its being perceived.' Here we are back to the 'obvious tho' amazing truth', for §6 begins:

Some truths there are so near and obvious to the mind, that a man need only open his eyes to see them. Such I take this important one to be, to wit … that all the bodies which compose the mighty frame of the world, have not any subsistence without a mind, that their being is to be perceived or known ...

A version of the above (master) argument is used for a more limited purpose by Berkeley in *De Motu* (1721), his chief work in the philosophy of science. Here he says that the idea of one body moving in absolute, empty space is a fiction that is given illegitimate credence by the fact that we project our own body into such a scenario without recognizing it.

> We are sometimes deceived by the fact that when we imagine the removal of all other bodies, yet we suppose our own body to remain. On this supposition we imagine the movement of our limbs fully free on every side ... no motion can be understood without some determination or direction, which in turn cannot be understood unless besides the body in motion our own body also, or some other body, be understood to exist at the same time ... So that if we suppose the other bodies were annihilated and, for example, a globe were to exist alone, no motion could be conceived in it ... (§§55, 58)

So once again, x cannot be perceived or understood by itself (divided from y); hence it does not exist. Yet here Berkeley is also trying to help us appreciate why we are mistakenly inclined to believe that one body can move in absolute space, by providing a genetic explanation for our false belief: that we unknowingly smuggle in our own body.

In *Principles*, §§18 and 20, he offers another thought

experiment, but unlike most of those we have considered, it is aimed not at proving that something does not exist; nor is it genetic or therapeutic as in the above statement from *De Motu*; rather it is designed to help us appreciate the feasibility of his immaterialism, by showing us how it might be possible. For

> ... it is granted on all hands (and what happens in dreams, phrensies, and the like puts it beyond dispute) that it is possible we might be affected with all the ideas we have now, though no bodies existed without, resembling them ... In short, if there were external bodies, it is impossible we should ever come to know it; and if there were not, we might have the very same reasons to think there were that we have now. Suppose, what no one can deny possible, an intelligence, without the help of external bodies to be affected with the same train of sensations or ideas that you are, imprinted in the same order and with like vividness in his mind. I ask whether that intelligence hath not all the reason to believe the existence of corporeal substances, represented by his ideas, and exciting them in his mind, that you can possibly have for believing the same thing? ... (PHK, §§18, 20)

Indeed, this thought experiment should probably have more impact at the present time, given developments in computer-generated experiences, than in Berkeley's day, since what he is suggesting is basically what is now called virtual reality. Thus anyone who wishes to see how flat patches or points of colour can appear to be three-dimensional, need only look at one of the ingenious, computer-generated stereograms.[7]

Another experiment used by Berkeley which goes further than that in *Principles*, §§18 and 20, but cannot be regarded as an experiment of proof or disproof (as are those in §§ 10 or 22–3), is the problem of the blind man made to see, the Molyneux problem. Although it was William Molyneux and not Berkeley who devised it, and although it was first printed by Locke in his *Essay* II.IX.8, it was Berkeley who uses it most effectively. (This may be said about most of his experiments, that although he did not devise them, he usually makes more interesting philosophical use of them than the devisers.) Indeed it is possible that it was the Molyneux problem that inspired Berkeley's interest in thought experiments. He touches on it again and again in his *New Theory of Vision* (and also in the PCs), but it is quoted and examined in detail in §§ 132–3, 135:

132 A farther confirmation of our tenet may be drawn from the solution of Mr Molyneux's problem, published by Mr Locke in his *Essay*: Which I shall set down as it there lies, together with Mr. Locke's opinion of it, ' "Suppose a man born blind, and now adult, and taught by his touch to distinguish between a cube and a sphere of the same metal, and nighly of the same bigness, so as to tell, when he felt one and t'other, which the cube and which the sphere. Suppose then the cube and sphere placed on a table, and the blind man to be made to see: *Quaere*, Whether by his sight, before he

26

touched them, he could now distinguish and tell which is the globe, which is the cube?" To which the acute and judicious proposer [Molyneux] answers: "Not. For though he has obtained the experience of how a globe, how a cube, affects his touch, yet he has not yet attained the experience that what affects his touch so or so must affect his sight so or so: Or that a protuberant angle in the cube that pressed his hand unequally shall appear to his eye as it doth in the cube." I agree with this thinking gentleman, whom I am proud to call my friend, in this answer to this his problem; and am of opinion that the blind man at first sight would not be able with certainty to say which was the globe which the cube, whilst he only saw them.' (*Essay* ... B. ii. C. 9 §8).

133 Now, [comments Berkeley] if a square surface perceived by touch be of the same sort with a square surface perceived by sight, it is certain the blind man here mentioned might know a square surface as soon as he saw it: it is no more but introducing into his mind by a new inlet an idea he has been already well acquainted with. ... We must therefore allow either that visible extension and figures are specifically distinct from tangible extension and figures, or else that the solution of this problem given by those two thoughtful and ingenious men [Locke and Molyneux] is wrong.

135 ... In short, the ideas of sight are all new perceptions, to which there be no names annexed in his mind: he cannot therefore understand what is said to him concerning them: And to ask of the two bodies he saw placed on the table which was the sphere, which

the cube? were to him a question downright bantering and unintelligible; nothing he sees being able to suggest to his thoughts the idea of body, distance, or in general of any thing he had already known.

So Berkeley takes his chief tenet to be confirmed, if the 'ingenious' Molyneux and Locke are right that the blind man made to see will not be able to identify the sphere and cube. Yet Berkeley also makes a conceptual point, that Locke's negative answer is inconsistent with his own theory that there are ideas (such as shape) common to what we see and touch.

As we have seen, Berkeley was delighted to be able to draw not merely testimonial but experimental confirmation of his tenet and his negative solution to Molyneux's problem from Cheselden's 1728 account of the boy couched for cataracts. And it was probably his wish to see Cheselden's case as corroborating his solution that initially made him misdescribe the boy as being blind from birth (in line with Molyneux's formulation) rather than infancy. Undoubtedly, Cheselden's patient supports a negative answer. He also probably supports Berkeley's more radical claim, or prediction, that not only will a newly sighted person be unable to distinguish by sight a cube from a sphere, but he will regard the question as unintelligible. For 'When he [the boy] first saw ... he could *form no judgement* of their [visual objects'] shape ...' (TVV, § 71, my italics).

Berkeley also uses Molyneux's problem more generally to make us appreciate the world from the perspective of the blind person made to see. And it may have been in this context that Berkeley was eventually able to make the *observation* that, although the question: 'Which is the sphere and which the cube?' will be 'unintelligible' to the newly sighted man, it may still be meaningful in a wider pragmatic sense. For in the *New Theory of Vision*, §148 Berkeley has this related thought experiment:

> Suppose one who had always continued blind be told by his guide that after he has advanced so many steps he shall come to the brink of a precipice, or be stopped by a wall; must not this to him seem very admirable and surprizing? He cannot conceive how it is possible for mortals to frame such predictions as these, which to him would seem as strange and unaccountable as prophesy doth to others. Even they who are blessed with the visive faculty may (though familiarity make it less observed) find therein sufficient cause of admiration. The wonderful art and contrivance wherewith it is adjusted to those ends and purposes for which it was apparently designed, ... may, ... give us some glimmering, analogous praenotion of things which are placed beyond the certain discovery and comprehension of our present state.

Here a blind person is told about visual things which he cannot conceive; therefore such words must be unintelligible or cognitively empty for him. And yet, by virtue of the experimental proof offered by his 'guide', he is able to accept that there are visual things and be full of admiration. Berkeley then suggests that this can help us to gain some notion of religious mysteries. Now consider an important entry from his notebooks, the *Philosophical Commentaries* (*c.* 1706–7), no. 720, where he speaks of a 'popish peasant' who can derive much edification from his Latin mass even though he does not understand it. For when it is a matter of words relating to Revelation and mystery, Berkeley says,

> an Humble Implicit faith becomes us just (where we cannot comprehend & understand the proposition) such as a popish peasant gives to propositions he hears at Mass in Latin. This proud men call blind, popish, implicit, irrational. For my part I think it more irrational to pretend to dispute at cavil & ridicule holy mysteries … that are altogether … above our knowedge out of our reach.

In short, Berkeley was, as I have elsewhere argued, on the verge here of his revolutionary non-cognitive, emotive theory of meaning: that words may be meaningful, even if they do not inform, provided they evoke appropriate emotions, attitudes or actions.[8]

In his use of the Molyneux problem and the thought experiment in §148 Berkeley is asking us to stretch our thinking. But it is at the end of the *New Theory of Vision* that he makes an even greater demand on our philosophical empathy. Here, conversely, we are asked to put ourselves in the position not of a blind person but of an unbodied mind that has *only* sight. As this is crucial for Berkeley's experimental approach, I quote it at length.

> … consider the case of an intelligence, or unbodied spirit, which is supposed to see perfectly well, i.e. to have

a clear perception of the proper and immediate objects of sight, but to have no sense of touch. Whether there be any such being in nature or no is beside my purpose to inquire. It sufficeth that the supposition contains no contradiction in it. Let us now examine what proficiency such a one may be able to make in geometry ...

154   First, then, it is certain the aforesaid intelligence could have no idea of a solid, or quantity of three dimensions, which followeth from its not having any idea of distance. We indeed are prone to think that we have by sight the ideas of space and solids, which ariseth from our imagining that we do, strictly speaking, see distance and some parts of an object at a greater distance than others; which have been demonstrated to be the effect of the experience we have had, what ideas of touch are connected with such and such ideas attending vision: but the intelligence here spoken of is supposed to have no experience of touch ... Whence it is plain he can have no notion of those parts of geometry which relate to the mensuration of solids ...

155   ... Nor it is an easier matter for him to conceive the placing of one plain or angle on another, in order to prove their equality: Since that supposeth some idea of distance or external space. All which makes it evident our pure intelligence could never attain to know so much as the first elements of plain geometry ...

156   All that is properly perceived by the visive faculty amounts to no more than colours, with their variations and different proportions of light and shade: But the

perpetual mutability and fleetingness of those immediate objects of sight render them incapable of being managed after the manner of geometrical figures ...

157   I must confess men are tempted to think that flat or plain figures are immediate objects of sight, though they acknowledge solids are not. And this opinion is grounded on what is observed in painting, wherein (it seems) the ideas immediately imprinted on the mind are only of plains variously coloured, which by a sudden act of the judgement are turned into solids: But with a little attention we shall find the plains here mentioned as the immediate objects of sight are not visible but tangible plains. For when we say that pictures are plains, we mean thereby that they appear to the touch smooth and uniform. But then this smoothness and uniformity, or, in other words, this plainess of the picture, is not perceived immediately by vision: For it appeareth to the eye various and multiform.

159   ... it is, indeed no easy matter for us to enter precisely into the thoughts of such an [unbodied sighted] intelligence, because we cannot without great pains cleverly separate and disentangle in our thoughts the proper objects of sight from those of touch which are connected with them. This, indeed, in a compleat degree seems scarce possible to be performed: Which will not seem strange to us if we consider how hard it is for anyone to hear the words of his native language pronounced in his ears without understanding them. Though he endeavour to disunite the meaning from the sound, it will nevertheless intrude into his thoughts, and

he shall find it extreme difficult, if not impossible, to put himself exactly in the posture of a foreigner that never learned the language, so as to be affected barely with the sound themselves, and not perceive the signification annexed to them.

Berkeley's initial, specific use of this psychological experiment is to determine whether the object of geometry is visual or tangible, but he then employs it to determine what we immediately and directly see. The Molyneux problem is another, somewhat narrower way of attempting to understand this; trying to imagine what a newborn infant sees would be still another way. Berkeley's thesis is that what the disembodied sighted mind would see is a visual field of mutable coloured points. There is no visual object that undergoes alterations or changes in shape, size, colour, etc., hence the sighted mind could have no notion of visual shape or size. Put in another way: there would be no shape or size constants for such a perceiver. We think we have them when we see, because our visual experiences have been frequently associated and connected with tangible ones. As a consequence, when we see something we imagine it to be tangible. Really, what we immediately see is as sizeless and shapeless as what the sighted mind sees; it is only a flux of light or colour points.

Within Berkeley's metaphysics this insight can be expressed in this way: what the sighted mind sees (and what we *immediately* see) is non-representational, non-linguistic, because for Berkeley (normal) vision is a language whereby God tells us about the tangible world. But prior to having experience of the tangible world, the visual language would be as meaningless as an utterly alien language. It would convey no meaning to the sighted mind. It is hard for us to appreciate this, Berkeley observes, because having learned the visual language, a powerful synesthesia, as it has come to be called, develops between the visual and tangible such that the visible object seems, or is imagined, to be tangible. Hence we believe that there is a necessary connection between what we see and touch, or that we actually see a tangible object. Berkeley takes this to be deeply mistaken. Here, unusually, he argues that x *can* be psychologically divided from y, that the visual is entirely separable from the tangible, and that it is we who have mentally conflated or united them.

What underpins this claim is Berkeley's *observation* that it is very difficult to hear words spoken in a familiar language without understanding what they mean (see NTV, §159; see also §51); and that it would be even more difficult if the familiar language (like vision) was virtually universal. Similarly, it is very hard *not* to read meaning into what we see, that is, to see the visual as such. Locke had moved in the direction of this insight with his discussion of depth perception in *Essay* II. IX. 8, preceding the Molyneux problem; and Berkeley may well be alluding to him in the *New Theory of Vision*, §157, for Locke showed that what we immediately see was not solid or three-dimensional. But Berkeley believes that we need to go further, that what we immediately see is not even flat shapes. This, Berkeley recognizes, is more difficult to accept. Yet just as it is hard for me to see my computer keyboard as purely visual, as

34

points of light and colour, rather than a flat surface with well-formed shapes that I recognize to be keys, so it is hard for me to hear my friend's words as just sounds. Yet, it is clear that I must first hear his pure sounds before I can understand his words (unless, perhaps, one wishes to posit some kind of telepathy).

So just because x (the visual keyboard, say) has been closely and frequently associated with y (the tangible keyboard), such that the two have become conflated, does not show that they are someone. For one might with practice be able to separate the two. As J. S. Mill pointed out in a similar context: 'a [psychological] difficulty is not an impossibility'.[9] (Of course this principle might be used against some of Berkeley's experiments, mentioned above, which try to show that x cannot be divided from y, for example extreme heat from pain.)

So it is essential for Berkeley to bring us as close as possible to the visual experience of the unbodied sighted mind, as it should help us to appreciate what we immediately see. To this end, I suggested above, a modern reader might be helped by looking at computer-generated stereograms, or at other forms of virtual reality. Another technique would be to suppose (as Roald Dahl does in his story called 'William and Mary') that in order to evade death, one has had one's brain put in a vat, and that the brain has one eye connected to it. Now suppose that someone moves your brain and eye about, and try to imagine the display of colours and light.

A warning, however, seems in order. Trying to put oneself in the position of the brain and eye, or Berkeley's more theological disembodied sighted mind, could be disorientating or even dangerous, since getting into that mode of perception might interfere with the normal one. It will be a very different world for such a perceiver, who will not have, as Berkeley believes, any notion of size or shape, since it has no grasp of position; indeed, it is unlikely that it will even have a notion of thingness. So although its grasp of the visual world may be truer, it will be virtually useless and hence probably indistinguishable from that of a blind person. In short, having deconstructed the visual world to its immediate sensations, a thought-experimenter might find it hard to return fully to our useful but fictitious (according to Berkeley) world of synthesized visual/tangible objects.

That Berkeley himself went very far in this experiment, despite its difficulties and dangers, seems evident from what he was able to bring back. There is also some evidence that he tried to do the above experiment not only for vision, but also for the senses individually. Thus his brief but confident description in *Principles*, §1, of the immediate data of the five senses, and especially that of touch, suggests first-hand experience: 'By touch [he says] I perceive, for example, hard and soft, heat and cold, motion and resistance, and of all these more and less either as to quantity or degree.' Moreover, in his essay no. 27 in the *Guardian* (1713), Berkeley considers the following:

Let us suppose a person blind and deaf from his birth, who, being grown to man's estate, is by the dead palsy or some other cause, deprived of his feeling, tasting, and smelling; and at the same time has the impediment of his hearing removed, and the film taken from his eyes. What the five senses are to us, that the touch, taste and smell were to him. And any other ways of perception of a more refined and extensive nature, were to him as inconceivable, as to us those are which will one day be adapted to perceive those things which *eye hath not seen, nor ear heard, neither hath it entred into the heart of man to conceive.* And it would be just as reasonable in him to conclude, that the loss of those three senses could not possibly be succeeded by any new inlets of perception; as in a modern free-thinker to imagine there can be no state of life and perception without the senses he enjoys at present. Let us further suppose the same person's eyes, at their first opening, to be struck with a great variety of the most gay and pleasing objects, and his ears with a melodious consort of vocal and instrumental music: Behold him amazed, ravished, transported; and you have some distant representation, some faint and glimmering idea of the exstatic state of the soul in that article in which she emerges from this sepulchre of flesh into Life and Immortalilty.

Here, as with the thought experiment in *New Theory of Vision*, §148 (quoted above), the aim is to give the reader some glimmering notion of the mysterious aspects of religion.

This thought experiment also helps to make sense of Berkeley's claim in his important letter of 1729 to his American friend, Samuel Johnson, that

I see no difficulty in conceiving a change of state, such as is vulgarly called Death, as well without as with material substance. It is sufficient for that purpose that we allow sensible bodies, i.e. such as are immediately perceived by sight and touch ... Now, it seems very easy to conceive the soul to exist in a separate state (i.e. divested from those limits and laws of motion and perception with which she is embarrassed here), and to exercize herself on *new ideas*, without the intervention of these tangible things we call bodies. (*Works* II, 282, my italics)

Yet Berkeley went further in trying to understand the mystery of death. This is the most dramatic experiment he carried out, showing the deadly seriousness of his experimentalism. It is recorded in the earliest (1759) biographical essay on him, by Oliver Goldsmith, who describes how Berkeley had himself hung by a college friend 'to know what were the pains and symptoms ... felt upon such an occasion'. The arrangement was that

his companion [Goldsmith's uncle, would] take him down at a signal agreed upon ... Berkeley was therefore tied up to the ceiling, and the chair taken from under his feet, but soon losing the use of his senses, his companion it seems waited a little too long for the signal agreed upon, and our enquirer [Berkeley] had like to have been hanged in good earnest; for as soon as he was taken down he fell senseless and motionless upon the floor.[10]

It is not entirely clear what Berkeley hoped to gain from this nearly fatal Near Death Experience – or NDEs as they

38

are now called. But it is likely that it was related to his suggestion (above) that death involves a total change in perceptions. Thus, in trying to experience the sensations immediately preceding death, Berkeley may have been testing to see whether he perceived totally new ideas, as he was emerging from the 'sepulchre of flesh'.

Apart from experimenting with a NDE, Berkeley also considered, more fancifully, the other main area of parapsychological investigation of death, that is OBEs, or Out of Body Experiences. For in another essay in the *Guardian*, no. 35, Berkeley tells of a philosopher who found a way 'for separating the soul for some time from the body, without any injury to the latter [thereby enabling the soul] to transport herself ... wherever she pleases, [for example] into the pineal gland of the most learned philosopher ...' By taking a philosophical snuff, Ulysses Cosmopolita, i.e. Berkeley, was able to enter into the minds of a freethinker and a critic in order to observe their ideas. It is, however, hard to know how seriously Berkeley thought about OBEs, even though it is certain he believed that the soul can exist in 'a separate state'.

Yet there can be no doubt about the seriousness of the next and final thought experiment I shall examine. It is probably Berkeley's most important and radical – that of the solitary man or philosopher, who thinks without language. In its own way, it is as daring as the unbodied sighted spirit and even his hanging experiment. Berkeley develops the experiment at length in the *Manuscript Introduction* (*c.* 1708) to the *Principles*, where it is presented as the guiding principle of his philosophical researches. In the published version it is much reduced, but the main point – that the philosopher should try to operate without language – remains. I quote from the more detailed *Manuscript* version:

> Let us conceive a solitary man, one born and bred in such a place in the world, and in such circumstances, as he shall never have had occasion to make use of universal signs for his ideas. That man shall have a constant train of particular ideas passing in his mind. Whatever he sees, hears, imagines, or any wise conceives is on all hands, even by the patrons of abstract ideas, granted to be particular. Let us withall suppose him under no necessity of labouring to secure him self from hunger and cold: but at full ease, naturally of good faculties and contemplative. Such a one I should take to be nearer the discovery of certain great and excellent truths yet unknown, than he that has had the education of the schools, … and by much reading and conversation has attain'd to the knowledge of those arts and sciences, that make such a noise in the learned world. It is true, the knowledge of our solitary philosopher is not like to be so very wide and extended, it being confin'd to those few particulars that come within his own observation. But then, if he is like to have less knowledge, he is withall like to have fewer mistakes than other men …
>
> I shall therefore endeavour as far as I am able, to take off the mask of words, and obtain a naked view of my own particular ideas, from which I may expect to derive the following advantages.

First, I shall be sure to get clear of all controversies purely verbal ...

Secondly, 'tis reasonable to expect that hereby the trouble of sounding, or examining, or comprehending any notion may be very much abridg'd. For it oft happens that a notion, when it is cloathed with words, seems tedious and operose and hard to be conceiv'd, which yet being strip't of that garniture, the ideas shrink into a narrow compass, and are view'd almost by one glance of thought.

Thirdly, I shall have fewer objects to consider, than other men seem to have had ...

Fourthly, having remov'd the veil of words, I may expect to have a clearer prospect of the ideas that remain in my understanding.

Fifthly, this seemeth to be a sure way to extricate myself out of that fine and subtile net of abstract ideas, which has so miserably perplex'd, and entangled the minds of men ...

Sixthly, so long as I confine my thoughts to my own ideas divested of words, I do not see how I can easily be mistaken. The objects I consider I clearly and adequately know. I cannot be deceiv'd in thinking I have an idea which I have not. Nor, on the other hand, can I be ignorant of any idea that I have. ...

But the attainment of all these advantages does presuppose an entire deliverance from the deception of words, which I dare scarce promise my self. So difficult a thing it is, to dissolve a union so early begun, and confirm'd by so long a habit as that betwixt words and ideas.

... I earnestly desire that every one would use his utmost endeavours to attain to a clear and naked view of the ideas he would consider, by separating them from all that varnish and mist of words, which so fatally blinds the judgement ...

Unless we take care to clear the first principles of knowledge from the incumbrance & delusion of words, we may make infinite reasonings upon them to no purpose. We may deduce consequences, and never be the wiser ... (MI, pp. 115–25)

There are interesting connections between this non-linguistic experiment and that of the sighted, unbodied mind. Here the attempt is made to perceive and think without words; in the former the aim was to see the visual as mere (visual) words, without any ideas or meanings. So just as it is hard for us to separate objects from words, so it is hard to perceive (God's visual) words without ideas – that is, once one has learned the relevant languages. Comparing the two thought experiments also reveals a curious conflict. Berkeley suggests that the solitary man is without language, but this cannot really be so if he is normally sighted, for then he will at least have the visual language.

The thought experiment of the solitary philosopher returns us nearly full circle to our starting point: Berkeley's critique of abstraction and language in the Introduction to the *Principles*. For it was his recognition of the perniciousness of language, of its fertile capacity to produce or reify fictions, that determined him to embark on this attempt to do philosophy without language. Berkeley's proposal is radical, yet it was by no means *sui generis*. Rather, it represents a culmination of an anti-linguistic tendency in philosophy that, although largely submerged, goes back at least to Plato (Epistle VII), one of Berkeley's heroes. About this negative view of language, Berkeley says in the *Manuscript Introduction*: 'Of late many have been very sensible of the absurd opinions, and insignificant disputes, that grow out of the abuse of words. ... to redress these evils, they advise well that we attend to the ideas that are signified and draw of our attention from the words that signify them' (p. 123). For Berkeley, however, it is not just that philosophical language can be pathological and in need of therapy – as those in the more recent Wittgensteinian tradition would hold – but that language is virtually always pathological; hence the solution is to move as fast and far as possible from language to experience, from linguistic to experimental or psychological philosophy.

In order to know that we are not in the linguistic maze, we need to determine, according to Berkeley, whether the things we are talking about exist; hence we need to look for the relevant perceptions. For him, this usually means retiring into himself and trying to imagine whether x exists, having formed the best definition possible of x. This is what he insists on again and again. The philosopher must do armchair psychology. For armchair psychology is hands-on philosophy. At one level, Berkeley's method could hardly be simpler – the psychological philosopher need only see if he can experience x, or experience x without y, or x with y. So it is simply a matter of 'compounding and dividing' (PHK, Intro. 10), or subtraction and addition. Yet Berkeley's results are anything but obvious, since on the basis of his experiments he maintains that abstract general entities, such as triangle, number and time, primary qualities such an extension and solidity, physical objects unperceived, tangible objects seen at a distance, are all fictions.

What Berkeley's experiments seem to show is that we live largely in a world of fictions created by language and imagination. Hence his stirring exclamation in his notebooks: 'Tis not to be imagined what a marvellous emptyness and scarcity of ideas that man shall descry who will lay aside all use of words in his meditations.' (PC, no. 600 and MI, p. 119). Yet Berkeley does not entirely condemn the fictions, for he believes that at least some of them are useful in ordinary life and even in science. In philosophy, however, he believes it is a different matter: *qua* philosophers, we ought to *'think with the learned, and speak with the vulgar'* (PHK, §51). But most speech is vulgar, generating fictions. Learned thinking is meditating, in the first instance, on particular perceptions, which for Berkeley are the things themselves.

Here we come to the chief difficulty in Berkeley's experimental method, which, at one level, appears so easy. For the Berkeleian philosopher, aiming to see the things themselves, has to see with his own external and internal eyes. He needs to be not only a careful observer, so that he can see, remember and imagine things accurately and in detail, but he needs to be sure of what he is perceiving. And this is harder than it sounds, for it is not at all easy to judge appearances and perceptions. After all, what nearly all adult people believe they perceive are solid, coloured objects at a distance. Berkeley would dispute this. But so, in an important sense, would most modern philosophers and scientists, since according to the scientific account accepted since the seventeenth century, what is really out there are clusters of particles or fields of energy, which, impinging on our sense organs, eventually produce in us or our brains the phenomena we experience. So what we perceive as the physical is structured by our modes of perceiving. Although this philosophical thesis is usually associated with Immanuel Kant, Berkeley agrees with it; although for him the structuring is more psychological than transcendental, more a matter of language and imagination than pure categories, and certainly not a matter of material brains and sense organs. What probably separates the Berkeleian most from either the Kantian or scientific account of perception is not that it is uncommonsensical – because they all are – but that Berkeley believes that individuals are able to unmask our ordinary, useful but fiction-laden judgements and experience things as they really are. Yet in order to do this, the philosopher needs to operate outside the normal sociolinguistic framework. Yet this, as I have noted, is not only difficult, but also potentially dangerous.

That Berkeley was aware of the dangers in moving outside the acceptable socio-linguistic matrix comes out in one of his sayings, recorded by his wife, Anne: 'His maxim [she writes] was that nothing very good or very bad could be done until a man entirely got the better of the fear of *que dira ton* [of what the fashionable world says] ...'[11] So working outside the consensual can result in something 'very good or very bad'. Berkeley himself does not seem to have been daunted by this. As he once said to his friend John Percival: 'I know not what it is to fear, but I have a delicate sense of danger.' That he was a courageous, perhaps even a rash, experimenter and observer can be seen in his willingness to hang himself and also in his close-up description of an eruption of Mount Vesuvius.

Of course, Berkeley's experimentalism involves more than courage; it also required gifts such as accurate and conscientious observation and memory, which he displays in his natural history works, and which are ascribed to him by acquaintances such as Blackwell. Equally important, Berkeley was a strong observer, able to see things that were camouflaged by familiarity, e.g., that the horizontal moon varied greatly in size. He was also able to observe things which went against the ingrained philosophical prejudices of the time, notably that people could use and be meaningfully affected by words which they did not understand, e.g., the popish peasant at his Latin mass.

These, of course, are largely abilities in outward observation. It is the inner observations that are crucial for the experimental philosopher and for two reasons: (1) external observations, such as those relating to the moon illusion, have been largely taken over by empirical psychology; and (2) introspection or subjective inner observation is now generally viewed with extreme suspicion. Of course, (2) was not always so. Until a century ago, probably most philosophers and psychologists, from Descartes to Mill, would have regarded inner observation as most certain. Nor is Berkeley's approach that foreign even to elements in twentieth-century science. Thus he is very much in line with Ernst Mach – who coined the term thought experiment (*Gedankenexperimente*) – in his sensationalist view of science and experiments, according to which the difference between real experiments and thought experiments is a matter of degree not kind. On this view, the problem of inner, first-person observations loses its sting, since the inner laboratory, according to Mach, is not essentially different from the outer.[12] Hence if someone has shown himself good in the outer, it seems only fair to suppose him good in the inner. This, I have been suggesting above, was generally the case with Berkeley. One way to underline this point is to look at whether the predictions he makes from thought experiments are then justified in the outward realm. Thus we can point to Berkeley's claim (in 1733) that his thought experiments of 1709 (about a blind man made to see) were publicly verified by Cheselden in 1728. It may also be relevant to mention in this respect that it has been claimed for Berkeley, by Karl Popper and others, that, particularly in *De Motu*, he strikingly anticipated developments in twentiety-century physics.[13]

Of course, for most present-day philosophers the problem of subjectivity, that is, the non-accessibility of first-person, subjective judgements, remains. Indeed for some philosophers, such as Gilbert Ryle and Daniel Dennett, the fact that only one person can fit into the subjective closet is evidence not only that such judgements are unreliable, but that they are spurious.[14] Nor was Berkeley unfamiliar with those who denied the existence of inner awareness and consciousness. In his *Guardian* essay, no. 130, he takes the following approach with such philosophers:

> The freethinkers have often declared to the world, that they are not actuated by any incorporeal being or spirit, but that all the operations they exert proceed from the collision of certain corpuscles, endued with proper figures and motions. It is now a considerable time that I have been their proselite in the point [namely that they are purely material] ... it being plain that no one could mistake thought for motion, who knew what thought was. For these reasons ... Christians [should] speak of [these] freethinkers in the neuter gender, using the term *it* for *him*. They are to be considered as *automata*, made up of bones and muscles, nerves, arteries and animal spirits ... but as destitute of thought ...[15]

What greater certainty could I have than that I am now thinking or having thoughts? For Berkeley, as for Descartes, there can be none. And I am inclined to agree. Similarly, can I seriously doubt that I am now hearing a hum (from my word processor)? Of course, under intense social, linguistic, or diabolical pressure, some people – including myself – might doubt their perceptions. Thus I might doubt – as Descartes did – that I am hearing, rather dreaming, a hum (although for Descartes and Berkeley I might still be sure that I was having an idea of humming). But I don't think I could doubt that I am now thinking. Yet I have heard students say that they were not certain that they existed at that moment.

One approach, following Berkeley, is not to dismiss the claims of Ryle, Dennett and these students. After all, how can I be certain that everyone is like me? Similarly it would be wrong of me to suppose that just because I can form private mental images, that everyone can. As Francis Galton and William James long ago showed, a small proportion of adults – and some of these extremely intelligent – are unable to form such visual images.[16] Berkeley's point is that it would be equally arrogant for these non-thinkers or non-image formers to claim that everyone is like them in the relevant respect. The temptation to pontificate in that way reveals a narrowness and unwillingness to see the world from another perspective.

Berkeley's life and philosophy goes directly against such narrowness, as is shown in his attempts to see the world from different points of view. Not everyone can empathize with alien perpectives. But there is evidence that Berkeley was especially good at putting himself into the minds – or, as with the above materialistic freethinkers, the non-minds – of his philosophical opponents. This is clear especially from his *Three Dialogues* and *Alciphron*, but it also comes out in a rare autobiographical reflection, where he noted to himself:

> He that would win another over to his opinion must seem to harmonize with him at first and humour him in his own way of talking. From my childhood I had an unaccountable turn of thought that way. (*Works* IX, 153)

But Berkeley the experimental philosopher was endowed

with more than merely a gift for good perceiving and imagining, more than courageous and strong observation and philosophical empathy. There is something, I suggest, which goes with and embraces these, namely, that the experimenter needs to understand himself. In one of his earliest extant letters, Berkeley describes this as 'a thing of the greatest advantage'. In this letter of 1709 to John Percival, he writes: 'There is a person whose acquaintance and conversation I do earnestly recommend unto you as a thing of the greatest advantage: you will be surprised when I tell you it is yourself.' Berkeley then suggests a simple regimen or exercise for moving towards self-knowledge, that is, 'to spend regularly and constantly two or three hours of the morning in study and retirement ... I do not take upon me to prescribe what you shall employ yourself about. I only propose the passing two or three hours of the twenty-four in private ...' (*Works* VIII, 20).

This encouragement to retirement and private meditation (and thereby self-understanding) would seem to be a modest form of Berkeley's chief methodological experiment, that of the solitary philosopher, who puts aside language for experience in the search for, and attainment of, truth. It is probably this proposal that would be greeted with the most horror and incredulity by present-day philosophers, who still largely believe that the revolution in philosophy, which I mentioned at the beginning of this volume, was a good thing, that it was right to oppose the psychological or mental science approach of J. S. Mill in favour of the conceptual and linguistic.

Now one curious feature of this opposition to the

psychological approach was that it united a wide range of philosophical enemies. Thus it was attacked by Hegelians, such as F. H. Bradley, by phenomenologists or existentialists, such as Edmund Husserl and Martin Heidegger, as well as by analytic philosophers, such as Gottlob Frege and Ryle.[17] Yet why such philosophical unanimity? The underlying answer, I believe, was the fear that psychology was about to absorb or take over philosophy. What psychology was that? It was the empirical psychology of Wilhelm Wundt and E. B. Titchener, who in the late nineteenth century set up laboratories in which teams of introspectors were used to examine questions relating to perception, concept formation, etc. One irony is that, in the event, that form of introspectionist psychology really posed little threat to philosophy, since it was largely swept away later in the twentieth century by behaviourism.[18]

A second irony is that philosophy is once again being threatened with absorption by psychology, but this time by de-subjectivised psychology, or psychology from a third-person perspective – for example, the so-called neuro-philosophy of Paul and Patricia Churchland, but more importantly by the naturalized epistemology of W. V. Quine.

Richard Rorty has summed up admirably in his *Contingency, Irony and Solidarity* (Cambridge, 1989) one main reason why philosophy as traditionally understood must be considered untenable. Basically, it follows from the growing recognition that the old notion of objective truth is illusory. 'To say that truth is not out there [writes Rorty] is simply to say that where there are no sentences there is no truth, that sentences are elements of human languages, and that languages are human creations … The suggestion that truth … is out there is a legacy of an age in which the world was seen as the creation of a being who had a language of his own …' (p. 5; see also p. 21).

Berkeley's answer to Rorty would be disarmingly simple: give up the central dogma that it is only within language that human understanding is possible and traditional philosophy ceases to be untenable. Of course, just because Berkeley's psychological philosophy would fulfil our wishes does not mean that it is true or feasible. For the question will naturally arise: has it not been refuted long ago along with that of his admirer, J. S. Mill? Clearly this question is too large to be satisfactorily answered here. But it is possible to sketch some Berkeleian answers.

First, it is not at all clear that human understanding is impossible without language. Admittedly, this seems to be widely accepted, both in Analytic and Continental circles; but that may be, as Ray Monk remarked to me, the dogma of the twentieth century. Before our century, most philosophers, including rationalists and empiricists, believed that thinking without language was entirely possible. To be sure, Berkeley goes further than most philosophers in holding that 'We need only draw the curtain of words, to behold the fairest fruit of knowledge'. Now one twentieth-century response to Berkeley is bound to be: 'Then describe what you see!' But this challenge supposes that one can only understand what one can communicate in some form of language. What is the evidence for that? In favour of non-linguistic understanding, a Berkeleian could point to the behaviour of pre-linguistic infants, who – to tailor Berkeley's description in Introduction §14 – seem to be able to play intelligently and make mental judgements about their rattles and sugar plumbs without the use of language.

Second, it might be said that the reasons psychology abandoned introspectionism in the early part of this century were and are equally valid for philosophy. Yet it is far from evident that they do bear on Berkeley's use of introspection. Wundt used many introspectionists operating over many trials to determine inductively the nature of human perception, concept formation, etc. Berkeley, however, uses it to discover the truth: to determine if, for example, extreme heat is inseparable from pain and hence is mind-dependent; to see if he can separate the visual and the tangible. Berkeley, unlike Wundt, was not looking for the normal or a standard. However, this is not to say that some psychological philosophers in the late nineteenth century did not see philosophy in a Wundtian way. Thus, according to Frege, Benno Erdmann equated truth with 'general validity' and 'general agreement between subjects who judge'.[19] But Berkeley, being utterly opposed to sceptical relativism, would never accept such a consensus criterion of truth – a criterion that is more in accord with the views of Rorty and, it would seem, of Quine.

For Berkeley, the true psychological philosopher is like an Olympic athlete: he is not interested in a norm, but in trying to find out what can or cannot be done. For this reason, the chief objection to Wundt's use of introspection, that it did not reach generally agreed results, does not apply to Berkeley.[20] As he puts it in the *New Theory of Vision*, in relation to the Molyneux problem: it is not a matter of finding out 'the sentiments of the generality of men' on this question, but of getting the considered judgement of a single unprejudiced person who performs the experiment.[21] In this respect, Berkeley would agree with the French philosopher Denis Diderot, who in his discussion of the Molyneux problem said that to carry out the experiment effectively 'would be an occupation worthy of the combined talents of Newton, Descartes, Locke and Leibniz'.[22]

Of course, even such an experimental philosopher could get it wrong. But so, presumably, could the philosopher or scientist operating within the consensus, from a third-person perspective. Clearly there is something safe and sensible in the latter approach; but taken to an extreme there is also something absurd in it. For in some sense, at least some or one of us have to see things in a first-person way, or we would be in the position of the behaviourist (in the well-known joke), who after having sex says to his behaviourist partner: 'That was nice for you. How was it for me?' At the very least, Berkeley's approach should be an antidote to this form of absurdity.

BERKELEY'S WORKS: EDITIONS AND ABBREVIATIONS

My quotations from Berkeley's writings are, with three exceptions, taken from *The Works of George Berkeley* (Edinburgh, 1948–57), A. A. Luce and T. E. Jessop (eds) in nine volumes. The three exceptions are: Berkeley's notebooks, or *Philosophical Commentaries* (Alliance, 1976), G. Thomas (ed.); Berkeley's *Manuscript Introduction* to the *Principles* (Oxford, 1987), B. Belfrage (ed.); and Berkeley's essays in Steele's *Guardian* (Kentucky, 1982), J. C. Stephens (ed.); quotations from which have been, where necessary, modernized and standardized.

PC *Philosophical Commentaries, c.* 1706–7

MI *Manuscript Introduction* to *Principles, c.* 1708

NTV *Essay Towards a New Theory of Vision* (1709; 4th edn 1732)

PHK (or *Principles*) *Principles of Human Knowledge* (1710; 2nd edn 1734)

DHP *Three Dialogues between Hylas and Philonous* (1713; 3rd edn 1734)

Alc. *Alciphron, or the Minute Philosopher* (1732; 3rd edn 1752)

TVV *Theory of Vision Vindicated and Explained* (1733)

Works *Works of George Berkeley* (1948–57), nine volumes.

NOTES

1. R. I. Watson and R. B. Evans, *The Great Psychologists: A History of Psychological Thought* (New York, 5th edn, 1991), p. 196.

2. J. S. Mill, 'Berkeley's Life and Writings', in Mill, *Collected Works*, Vol. vii, J. M. Robson (ed.), (Toronto, 1978), p. 451.

3. See G. Ryle, Introduction to *The Revolution in Philosophy* (London, 1965), especially pp. 4–8.

4. T. Blackwell, *Memoirs of the Court of Augustus* (Edinburgh, 1755), Vol. 2, pp. 277–8.

5. See L. Kaufman and I. Rock, 'The Moon Illusion', in *Perception: Mechanism and Models*, R. Held and W. Richards (eds.), (San Francisco 1950), pp. 260–8; D. Berman, 'Berkeley and the Moon Illusions', in *Revue Internationale de Philosophie* 154 (1985), pp. 215–22. Curiously, Voltaire, who carried out similar experiments using pasteboard tubes, came to results similar to Berkeley, that the illusion persists; see his *Elements of Newton's Philosophy*, Ch. vi.

6. J. Bennett, *Locke, Berkeley, Hume* (Oxford, 1971), pp. 91–2.

7. See, for example, *Magic Eye: A New Way of Looking at the World* (Harmondsworth, 1994), no. 22, and D. Dyckman, *Hidden Dimensions* (London, 1994).

8. See D. Berman, *George Berkeley: Idealism and the Man* (Oxford, 1994), pp. 12–16, 144–8.

9. J. S. Mill, 'Auguste Comte and Positivism', *Collected Works* Vol. x, J. M. Robson (ed.), (Toronto, 1969), p. 296.

10. See 'Memoirs of the late famous Bishop of Cloyne', in *Works of Oliver Goldsmith*, A. Friedman (ed.), (Oxford, 1966), Vol. 3, p. 35.

11. For this and the following quotation, see my *George Berkeley* (Oxford, 1994), p. 210.

12. See R. A. Sorenson, *Thought Experiments* (New York, 1992), Ch. 3.

13. K. Popper, 'A Note on Berkeley as Precursor of Mach', *British Journal for the Philosophy of Science* IV (1953), pp. 26–36.

14. See G. Ryle, *The Concept of Mind* (London, 1949); D. Dennett, *Consciousness Explained* (Harmondsworth 1993).

15. On this essay, see my *George Berkeley*, pp. 75–7.

16. See F. Galton, *Inquiries into Human Faculty and its Development* (London, 1911 edn), especially pp. 58–61, and W. James, *Principles of Psychology* (London, 1890), Vol 2, Ch. 18, where Galton is quoted at length.

17. See, e.g., *The Revolution in Philosophy* (London, 1965), especially Ryle's Introduction and the essays on Bradley·and Frege (by R. A. Wollheim and W. C. Kneale), pp. 3–6, 13–15, 31.

18. See D. N. Robinson, *An Intellectual History of Psychology* (Boston, 1996), Ch. 11, especially p. 306.

19. G. Frege, *The Basic Laws of Arithmetic* (Berkeley, 1967), M. Furth (trans.) pp. 13–14.

20. W. Lyons, *The Disappearance of Introspection* (Cambridge, Mass., 1986), Ch. 1.

21. See NTV, § 127, first edition.

22. See *Diderot's Early Philosophical Works* (Chicago, 1916), M. Jourdain (trans.), p. 118.

I am grateful to Dr Bertil Belfrage, Professor William Lyons and Dr Paul O'Grady for comments on an earlier draft of the essay.